PERGAMON INTERNATIONAL LIBRARY
of Science, Technology, Engineering and Social Studies
The 1000-volume original paperback library in aid of education,
industrial training and the enjoyment of leisure
Publisher: Robert Maxwell, M.C.

Initial Skills
in
BRICKLAYING
A Practical Guide

THE PERGAMON TEXTBOOK
INSPECTION COPY SERVICE

ERRATA

INITIAL SKILLS IN BRICKLAYING
P. Tempest

Page 35

Second line after illus. 36 should read:

    Numeral 2. Set out mortar spots . . . . . .

Page 80

The bricks shown in illus. 88 and 89 are incorrectly labelled and should
be transposed.

Page 93

Line 13 from the bottom should read "Flemish bond . . . ."

Other Pergamon Books for the Craftsman and Student

00006649

Prepared for Vocational and Non-vocational
Courses in Colleges, Training Centres, Workshops,
and for Self-teaching

Initial Skills

in

BRICKLAYING
A Practical Guide

P. J. Tempest
B.A., H.N.C., Bldg., M.G.B.
West Nottinghamshire College of Further Education,
England

Photographs Chris Locke
Illustrations Susan Burton

PERGAMON PRESS

Oxford   New York   Toronto
Sydney   Paris   Frankfurt

U.K.	Pergamon Press Ltd., Headington Hill Hall, Oxford OX3 0BW, England
U.S.A.	Pergamon Press Inc., Maxwell House, Fairview Park, Elmsford, New York 10523, U.S.A.
CANADA	Pergamon Press Canada Ltd, Suite 104, 150 Consumers Road, Willowdale, Ontario M2J 1P9, Canada
AUSTRALIA	Pergamon Press (Aust.) Pty. Ltd., P.O. Box 544, Potts Point, N.S.W. 2011, Australia
FRANCE	Pergamon Press SARL, 24 rue des Ecoles, 75240 Paris, Cedex 05, France
FEDERAL REPUBLIC OF GERMANY	Pergamon Press GmbH, 6242 Kronberg-Taunus, Hammerweg 6, Federal Republic of Germany

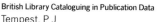

First edition 1981

British Library Cataloguing in Publication Data

Tempest, P J
Initial skills in bricklaying.
—(Pergamon international library).
1. Building, Brick
I. Title
693.2'1   TH1301   80-41756

ISBN 0 – 08 – 025424 – 1 Hardcover
ISBN 0 – 08 – 025423 – 3 Flexicover

Printed in Great Britain by A. Wheaton & Co., Ltd., Exeter

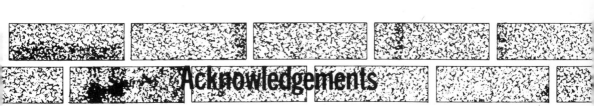

Acknowledgements

The author wishes to thank the following for their help in the preparation of this book:

Rita Bray
Butterley Building Materials Ltd.
Ian Cox M.C.I.O.B.
London Brick Company Limited
West Nottinghamshire College of Further Education
Albert Whitton
George Reynolds F.T.C., M.G.B., Cert Ed.

The author also expresses appreciation for the help and advice given on many points of bricklaying practice by Mr. Malcolm Thorpe, Lecturer in charge of the Brickwork Section at West Nottinghamshire College of Further Education.

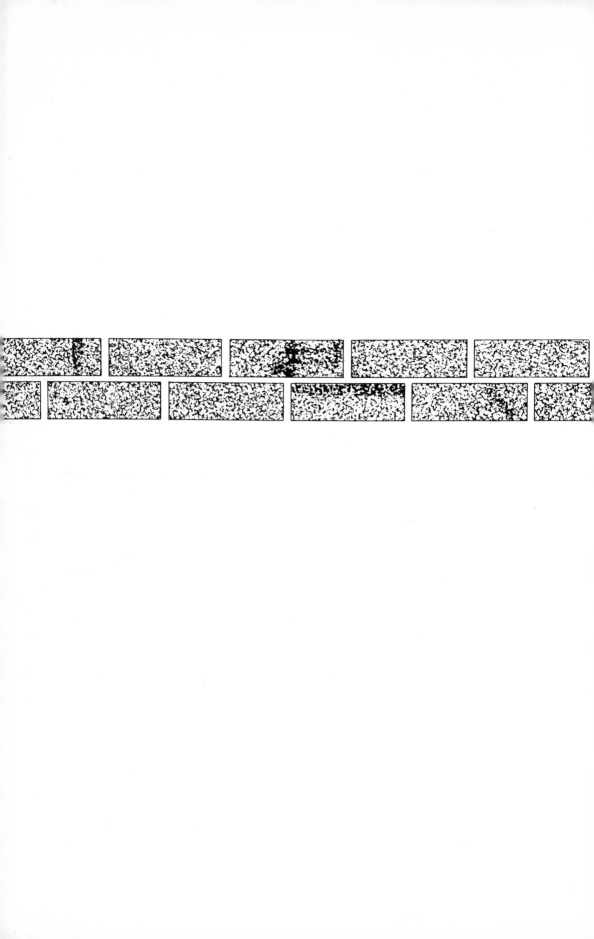

Contents

1 Introduction

THIS book has two main purposes. To offer a practical guide for teachers and to be a self-teaching guide for the person who would like to learn bricklaying. If the guide is followed reasonably closely and sufficient practice undertaken students should be able to undertake good-quality permanent work.

The first part of the book deals with terms used, standards of accuracy, use of tools, hand skills, practice exercises and models. The second part deals with blocklaying, more advanced hand skills, technical and general information and examples of permanent work which students could undertake.

Individual users will be able to apply the marking scheme which is suggested for the practice models to suit their own requirements; however, it is worthwhile in the learning of any skill to have some measure or criteria of achievement. With this in mind it is suggested that students check their own performance or have others check on their behalf using the marking schemes available and the performance criteria set out on page 11.

To learn the practical skills of bricklaying few tools and materials are required. A bricklaying trowel, spirit plumb level, lump hammer, bolster, bricklayer's line, chalk, gauge lath, line blocks, profiles, timber square and mortar spot boards are essential but in groups only the trowel, line and block profiles and mortar spot should not be shared. A brick hammer can be useful but is not essential.

The bricks and mortar for practice are re-usable and fifty bricks are sufficient for one student. The gauge lath, line blocks, square, profiles and mortar spot boards can be made from old timber.

A non-bricklayer wishing to use the book for teaching others will obviously need to practice the exercises prior to teaching but this should not present serious problems for the reasonably dextrous.

Bricklaying requires a high level of hand and eye co-ordination. The purpose of the practice exercises is to develop these skills to produce neat, accurate and attractive brickwork measured against given performance targets.

Practice models should be set out in an orderly manner bearing some geometric relationship as do the various parts of a building.

Abilities will vary but it is advised that good students are encouraged to develop higher levels of accuracy in finished work in preference to more intricate models. For less able students practice between profiles (see page 35) is beneficial.

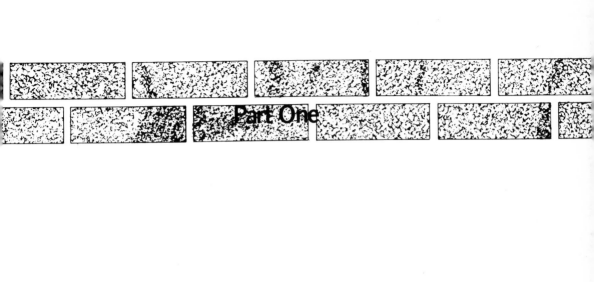

Part One

2 Bricklaying Tools

TROWEL – often has a straight edge on the left of the blade for a right-handed trowel and on the right of the blade for a left-handed trowel. This straight edge is an aid to picking up mortar clean from the mortar spot, for cutting surplus mortar from the bed and cross joints and for weather pointing.

The curved edge of the trowel blade is intended for tapping bricks down to the correct level and for rough cutting of bricks. Note that students should not use a trowel for cutting bricks until they are competent bricklayers.

Illustration 1

Right-handed bricklaying trowel

Not all trowels are of the same pattern, the American or Canadian trowel having both edges of the blade curved and some European trowels having rectangular or fully rounded blades. It is advisable to use standard sized bricklaying trowels until competence is achieved. This book assumes use of a pointed trowel.

Right- or left-handedness. The trowel is held in the dominant hand; the subdominant hand is used for handling the bricks. Where appropriate in this book the dominant hand and the subdominant hand are called the trowel hand and the brick hand respectively.

Rule – marked in millimetres, used in conjunction with spirit plumb rule for checking accuracy of plumb and level and for joint sizes and accurate cutting measurements.

Gauge lath – timber lath with saw cuts or other marks to indicate the height of each course of bricks and the mortar bed.

Illustration 2

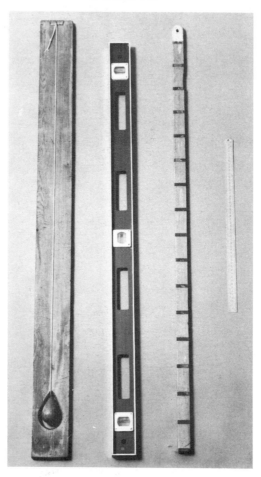

| Plumb rule | Plumb level | Gauge lath | mm rule |

Illustration 2 also shows a plumb rule made from timber, bricklayer's line and a metal weight. This method of plumbing is slower and requires more skill but would save buying a plumb level. For levelling a spirit-filled level tube fixed to a suitable lath or a manufactured boat level would be needed.

Spirit plumb level – bubble between the two black marks on the lower of the pair of bubbles shows plumb or level – used to check plumb (vertical) and level during construction and on completion of the work.

Illustration 2 cont.

Plumbing bubble of a plumb level

Levelling bubble of a plumb level

Lump hammer – 1-kg hammer used in conjunction with a bolster for cutting bricks.

Illustration 3

Lump hammer

Bolster—100mm-wide chisel. When cutting or trimming bricks the brick should rest on a fibre of soft wood pad to reduce unnecessary fractures. For final cutting the bolster should be given a sharp heavy blow with the lump hammer.

Illustration 4

Bolster

Bricklayer's line – usually a 1-mm-thick white cotton line – fixed at the height of the top face arris of the course of bricks being laid – used as a guide to positioning the bricks. The line is also used for chalking out.

Line blocks – shaped wooden blocks with saw cuts for fastening the brick-layer's line – fixed at the correct gauge for the course of bricks being laid and held in place by the tension of the line.

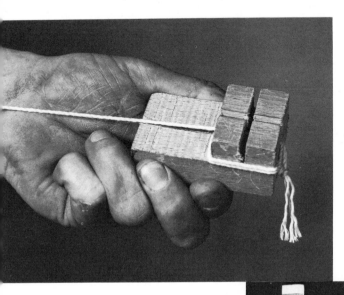

Illustration 5

Line block and bricklayer's line

Profiles — timber vertical 'square' with flat base – used as a training aid for plumbing and gauging.

Illustration 6

Profile with gauge marks

Square – timber square approximately 500 × 500 mm and braced – used for setting out and checking for squareness with the aid of a straight edge or plumb rule.

Illustration 7

Builder's square

Spot board – square timber boards or similar, approximately 500 × 500 mm, positioned at the place of work to hold mortar for immediate use.

Spotboard – top view   Spot board – view of underside

Brick hammer see page 84

Special clothes – boots or shoes with hard toe caps and protective goggles are advisable.

3 Bricklaying Terms

Course	horizontal row of bricks built into a wall.
Plumb	Vertical – checked by a spirit plumb level.
Level	Horizontal – checked by a spirit plumb level.
Gauge	height of each course of bricks and bed joint – checked with gauge lath.
Bed joint	horizontal mortar joint on which each course of bricks is laid – usually 10 mm thick and checked when the gauge lath is used for setting the first brick of a new course.
Cross joint	vertical mortar joint between each brick – checked by a suitable 10-mm-thick gauge, e.g. chalk.
Arris	the edge formed between any two adjacent sides of a brick.
Face plane	the vertical face of a wall on the working side.
Header	a brick laid with its end exposed on the face of the wall.
Stretcher	a brick laid with its length exposed on the face of the wall.
Closer	a brick cut vertically along its length.
Half-brick wall	a wall as thick as the width of one brick.
One-brick wall	a wall as thick as the length of one brick.
Frog	the recess in a brick.
Bond	the lapping of one brick over another so that cross joints do not occur one above the other.
Stretcher bond	half lapping one brick over another as in a half-brick wall – this is the most common modern bond used in cavity walls.
English bond	alternate courses of headers and stretchers with quarter-brick lapping of the cross joints.
Flemish bond	alternate headers and stretchers on the same course with quarter-brick lapping of the cross joints on the courses above and below and placing headers centrally over stretchers.

Quoin	the vertical angle formed between two face planes of brickwork.
Raking back	building up brickwork so that each course is one bond cross joint shorter than the course below.
Reveal	the vertical brickwork at the sides of openings through walls.
Ranging in	aligning the face plane of the brickwork with a straight edge, e.g. plumb level.

4 Standards for Brickwork

Good-quality face work

Suitable for high-class exposed brickwork.

Plumb
brickwork must be plumb to within 1 mm in 1 m of height and all bricks must touch the plumb level.

Bed and cross joints
average thickness and widths must be 10 mm with no deviation greater than 2 mm from the standard.

Gauge
no brick may deviate from gauge more than 1 mm at the gauge point.

Face plane
no brick may deviate from more than 1 mm face.

Appearance
brickwork must be free of mortar smudges, chipped bricks and badly cut halves or closures.

Illustration 8

Good-quality iron jointed facework using rusticated bricks in stretcher bond

Standard face work

Fair faced work. Suitable for exposed brickwork on domestic and industrial buildings.

Plumb	brickwork must be plumb within 2 mm in 1 m of height and no brick may be clear of the plumb level by more than 1 mm.
Bed and cross joints	average thicknesses and widths must be 10 mm with no deviation greater than 5 mm from the standard.
Gauge	no brick may deviate from gauge more than 3 mm at the gauge point.
Face plane	no brick may deviate from the face more than 4 mm.
Appearance	brickwork must be no more than minimally smudged, there must be no badly chipped bricks, halves or closures.

Common work

Work not usually directly visible, i.e. requiring a surface treatment such as paint or plaster.

Plumb	brickwork must be plumb within 4 mm in 1 m of height and no brick may be clear of the plumb level by more than 3 mm.
Bed and cross joints	average thicknesses and widths must be 10 mm with no deviation more than 10 mm from the standard for cross joints and 5 mm for the bed joints.
Gauge	no brick may deviate from gauge more than 5 mm at the gauge point.
Face plane	no brick may deviate from the face more than 6 mm.
Appearance	brickwork may be smudged and chipped and rough cutting is acceptable.

Unseen work

Foundations. Brickwork not seen and not given any surface treatment.

Plumb	brickwork may not exceed 10 mm from plumb within 1 m height and bricks may be clear of the plumb level by up to 5 mm.

Bed and cross joints	average thicknesses and widths must be 10 mm with no deviations more than 10 mm.
Gauge	brickwork must be within 10 mm of correct gauge at ten courses high.
Face plane	no brick may deviate from the face more than 10 mm.
Appearance	not critical.

5 Materials

Choice of bricks for practice

A wide range of bricks are available for general building work but for practice purposes a smooth uniformly shaped brick of consistent dimensions is most suitable. Smooth bricks are most easily cleaned for re-use. A uniform shape increases accuracy of working and allows careful checking as the work proceeds and on completion. Consistent dimensions help to maintain required thicknesses and width of bed and cross joint and improves the accuracy of gauging.

Good, smooth-faced wire cut, pressed fletton or calcium silicate (sand lime) common bricks are best.

Other bricks can be used but at first the speed of skill improvement will be reduced and the finished quality of the work will be less orderly and regular.

Mortar for practice

A mortar mix of 5 parts clean building sand and 1 part lime is suitable. The mixed mortar should be soft enough to spread easily with the back of the trowel blade to a 10-mm-thick bed joint but firm enough for a small quantity to adhere to the trowel when it is turned over.

The mortar can be re-used but care must be taken to stop brick chips from being mixed into the mortar. This will interfere with the bedding and jointing of the bricks.

A standard builder's mortar mixer can be used but a mortar mill with crushing rollers is most suitable in the case of permanent practice facilities. For low cost or short-term practice hand mixing with a builder's shovel is much the cheapest method of mixing the mortar.

6 Practice Exercises

Chalking a line

1. Choose a suitable space on an even surface where the spot boards and bricks can be set out along a straight line.
2. Using chalk, mark the ends of the intended materials setting out line.
3. Hold a bricklayer's line at a convenient height above and between these marks. Keeping the line tight, chalk it thoroughly by running the chalk two or three times along its length.

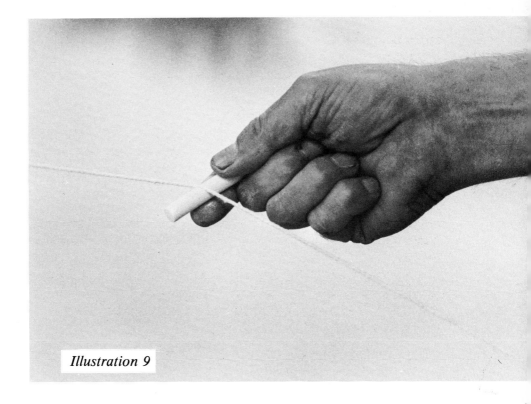

Illustration 9

4. Lower the line to the two end marks and hold under tension.

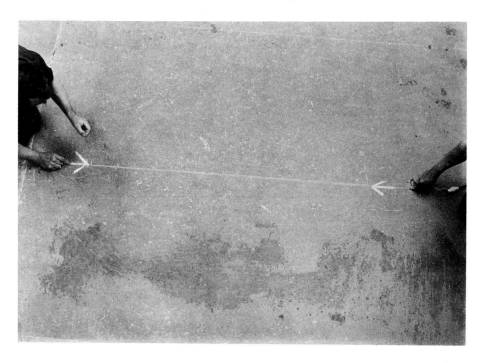

5. Raise the line vertically 300 mm at its centre and release, making sure the line strikes the ground direct.

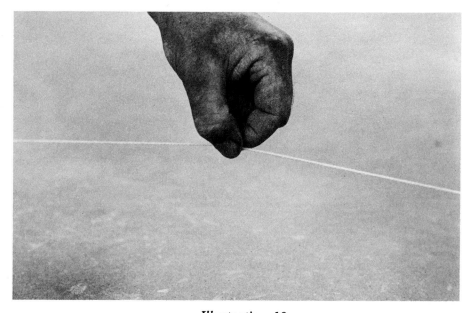

Illustration 10

Setting out materials

Exercise 1

The intention of this exercise, which should be repeated with suitable variation at the start of each group of models, is to emphasise from the outset the benefit of an orderly approach to setting out materials in the work-space.

1. Chalk a line as above.
2. Set out not less than two spot boards and two stacks of six bricks as illustrated diagramatically below. The spot boards should stand on four bricks placed symmetrically. Use bricks for measuring spacings.

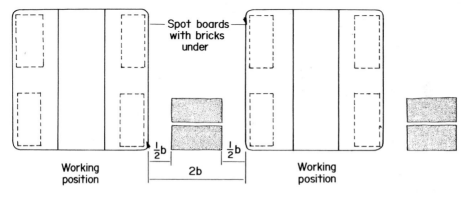

Illustration 11

Marking scheme	
Line of spots	2
Line of bricks	2
Space between spots	2
Spacing of brick stacks	2
Symmetry of support bricks	2
Total	10

By marking according to fine limits of accuracy students will be introduced to an emphasis on careful checking of work.

Using this diagrammatic layout younger students should gain some experience of interpreting simple representational drawings.

Handling trowel and mortar

Exercise 2. Cutting and rolling

1. Wet the spot boards with clean water.
2. Set two shovels of mortar on the spot boards.
3. Stand in the correct working position for picking up mortar, i.e. right-handed bricklayers forward and to the right facing the spot board, left-handed bricklayers reversed.
4. Cut away a quantity of mortar as shown.

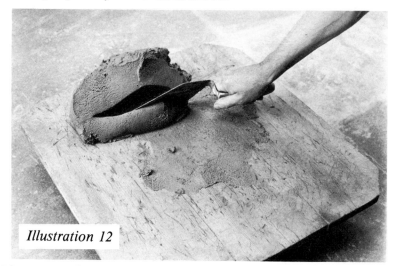

Illustration 12

5. Using a curved sawing stroke draw the trowel of mortar across the spot to form a roll.

Illustration 13

6. Move the trowel back from the roll of mortar and turn it so that the blade is horizontal, 1 mm above the spot board and 50 mm diagonally away from the roll.

Illustration 14

7. With a sharp movement pick up the roll of mortar.

Illustration 15

8. Set the trowel of mortar back with the rest on the spot board and repeat the cycle.

Marking scheme	
Correct working position	2
Handling of trowel	2
Neatness of cutting away	2
Cleaness of rolling	2
Accuracy of picking up	2
Total	10

Exercise 2 should be repeated, alternating with other hand skill exercises, until an easy, clean and accurate cycle is achieved by the student.

Spreading bed joints

Exercise 3.   Spread, furrow and cut off surplus

Start from stage 7, Exercise 2.

1. Hold trowel of mortar over the edge of the spot board.
2. In a sweeping movement draw the trowel parallel to and along the edge of the spot simultaneously turning the trowel blade and spreading the mortar along the edge of the spot board.

Illustration 16

3. With the trowel point, furrow the spread mortar along its length with a series of undulating trowel movements.

Illustration 17

4. Cut off the surplus mortar along the edge of the spot board to produce a clean edge to the spread mortar.

Illustration 18

5. Clear mortar from edge of spot and repeat.

Marking scheme	
Turning mortar off trowel	2
Mortar spread	2
Mortar furrow	2
Cutting off surplus	2
Thickness of cut edge	2
Total	10

It is important on this exercise to achieve a neat furrow, a clean cut where the surplus is removed and 12 mm average thickness of the bed joint at the edge. These features of spreading the bed joint are very important for easy, quick and accurate placing of the bricks on the mortar bed and for keeping the face of the bricks clean as they are laid.

Handling bricks

The subdominant hand is used for handling bricks; picking up, turning to the correct face or bedding plane, placing on the mortar bed and accurately aligning the bricks. This is a series of hand skills which may require some practice to develop to a satisfactory standard. If possible use a lighter deep frog brick for practice. The correct way to hold a brick is across its width. Protective footwear is advisable when handling bricks.

Exercise 4.   Turning a brick to the correct bedding plane

1.   Hold a brick across its width in the correct hand, i.e. if right-handed hold the brick in the left hand and the reverse if left-handed.

Illustration 19

2. At approximately waist level spin the brick along its longitudinal axis through half a rotation, the top of the brick rotating toward the thumb.

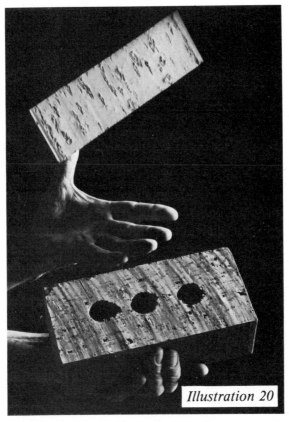

Illustration 20

3. Repeat until the brick has been spun through ten correct successive half turns without dropping.

Marking scheme	
One mark for each successful half turn	10
Total	10

This exercise is intended to improve the student's skill in turning a brick so that the correct bed is uppermost, e.g. frog up. It is essential that the brick is held across its width, that the turns are each a half rotation and that the student can catch the brick across its width. If two moves are required to achieve half a rotation the time taken is increased 100%.

Exercise 5. *Turning a brick to the correct face*

1. Hold a brick across its width in the correct hand as in Illustration 24.

2. At approximately waist height spin the brick along its lateral axis through half a rotation, top of the brick moving toward the body.

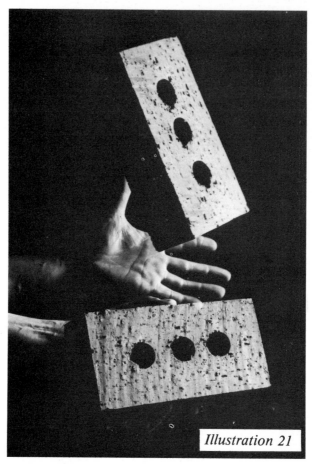

Illustration 21

3. Repeat until the brick has been spun through ten correct successive half turns without dropping.

This exercise is intended to improve the student's skill in turning a brick so that the correct face is exposed on the finished work, e.g. textured side out.

As in Exercise 4 correct holding, turning and catching of the brick is essential.

Applying cross joints

Before one brick is laid adjacent to another the cross joint must be filled. Experienced bricklayers will often do this *in situ* using the last brick laid. Students should mortar the cross joints of the brick to be laid as an aid to accurate bedding of the brick and as practice in co-ordination of hand movements.

Exercise 6. 'Buttering' bricks

1. Take a scoop of mortar on the trowel blade direct from the mortar pile on the mortar spot.

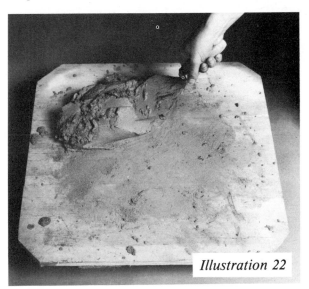

Illustration 22

2. Flex the wrist of the trowel hand firmly to cause the mortar to spread across and adhere to the trowel blade.

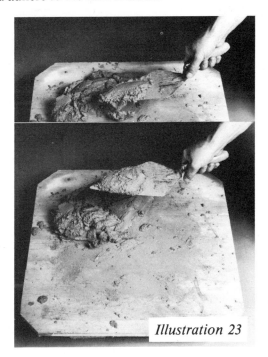

Illustration 23

3. Pick up a brick across its width. With the bedding plane toward the trowel hand hold the brick and the trowel in front of the body and just apart.

Illustration 24

4. Draw the trowel blade down across the width of the brick at its end so that a portion of the mortar on the blade is struck on to the brick.

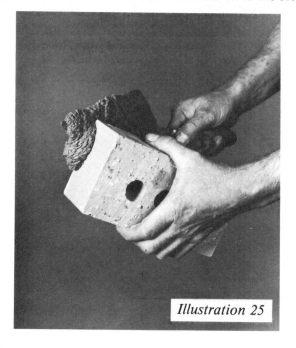

Illustration 25

5. Lift the trowel again and turn it through 90°. Draw the blade down across the face edge of the brick at its end. Again a portion of mortar should be struck on to the brick.

Illustration 26

Illustration 27

6. Move the trowel hand away from the body over the top of the brick. Push the trowel blade across the back edge of the brick. A third portion of mortar should be struck on to the brick.

7.   The brick should now be buttered on three arrises at its end, ready to lay.

Marking scheme	
Flexing wrist and spreading on blade	2
First movement	2
Second movement	2
Third movement	2
Finished buttering	2
Total	10

There are a number of ways of filling a cross joint. This method of 'buttering' a brick may be discontinued in preference for a more personal alternative when a high level of trowel skill is achieved.

The purpose of the exercise is to develop accurate simultaneous use of brick and trowel hands for a wider range of co-ordinated actions. The exercise should be repeated until the brick can be buttered in three quick successive movements so that no mortar falls from the brick or the trowel.

Use of bolster and lump hammer

Exercise 7. Cutting halves

1.   Set one brick face up on an offcut of timber or fibre board.
2.   Mark the face of the brick for cutting using the width of another brick as a guide.

Illustration 28

3. Hold the blade of the bolster on the face of the brick and vertical to it.
4. Strike the bolster with a firm hard blow with the lump hammer.

Illustration 28 cont.

5. Use the bolster and lump hammer to trim any excess remaining on the half brick.

Marking scheme	
Marking for cutting	2½
Holding bolster	2½
Striking bolster	2½
Accuracy of cut	2½
Total	10

This exercise should not be repeated except when half bricks are required. Once cut half bricks can be re-used. The cut portion of the brick is less than half the length of a brick. This allows for a cross joint when the half brick is bedded.

Exercise 8. Cutting closers

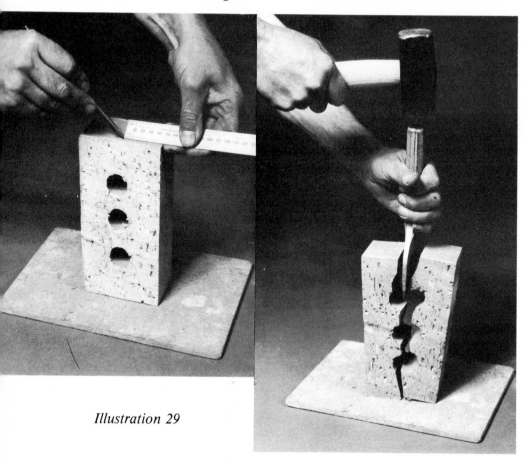

Illustration 29

1. Mark the line of cut for the closer on each header face of the brick to be cut. (Note that to maintain accurate bond and cross-joint position a closer is not always half a header.)
2. Stand the brick on one header face on a fibreboard pad and place the bolster along the cutting line.
3. Strike a medium blow with a lump hammer, turn the brick to the other header face and repeat the cut with one medium blow.
4. Continue, alternating between each header face until the brick is cut.

It is unusual to cut a closer successfully as illustrated at the first practice and with some types of bricks it will be difficult to produce a closer in a single piece after many attempts. With such bricks, or if attempts at cutting closers in a single piece are particularly unsuccessful, it is acceptable to use a closer which has broken in two.

7 Laying Bricks

Practice model 1

Illustration 30

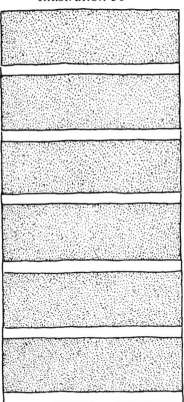

Front elevation of "stack"
bond model

1. Set out for practice exercise as on page 17.
2. Chalk a line three bricks in front of and parallel to the line of mortar spots.
3. Chalk the position of the model *central* in front of the mortar spots.

4. Lay a mortar bed as in Exercise 3, sufficient for one brick.

Illustration 31

5. Pick up and bed one brick in the position marked.
6. In conjunction with the gauge lath press the brick down to the gauge mark. Do not use the trowel hand for handling the brick.

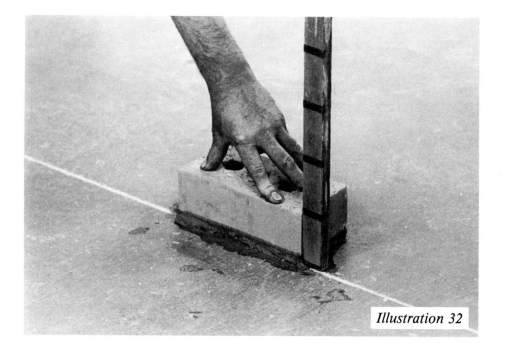

Illustration 32

7. By visual inspection only, check the brick for level and plumb and adjust as necessary.
8. Lay a second bed of mortar on the first layed brick and neatly trim the surplus away from the face of the brick.

Illustration 33

9. Pick up and bed a second brick, press the brick down to gauge and inspect. By sight only adjust for level, plumb and alignment. Cut off any further surplus mortar squeezed from the bed joint again by holding the trowel so that it cuts the mortar away from the face of the bricks.

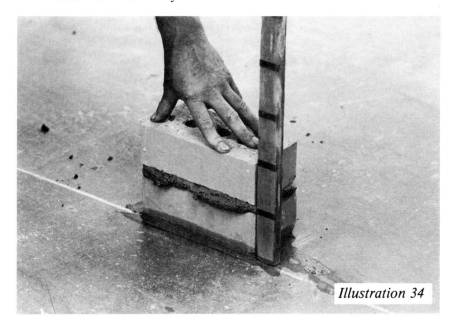

Illustration 34

10. Continue until six bricks are laid one on top of the other (stack bond).
11. Check the finished model for gauge, level and plumb using gauge lath and the plumb level on top, one side and the face. Note that bricks vary in length and if one side of the model is plumb and aligned the opposite side may not be.

Illustration 35

Marking scheme	
Accuracy of position of model in relation to mortar spot (setting out)	2
Gauge of each brick	2
Level	2
Plumb	2
Appearance	2
Total	10

The most important aspect of this model is the visual checking. Students should produce a model which is level, plumb and accurately aligned on the face and end elevation without the use of any aid.

It is important that the mortar bed is laid carefully, and to the correct thickness to avoid disturbing bricks already laid.

If the model curls over, twists or is otherwise misaligned it should be repeated.

Stack bond is unusual in brickwork and is used in this case only as an exercise.

Practice model 2   Half a brick wall to a line between profiles

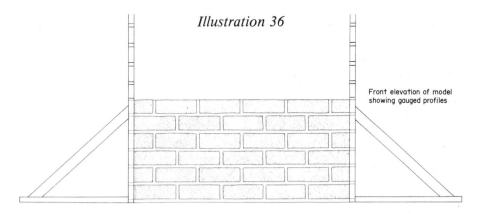

Illustration 36

Front elevation of model
showing gauged profiles

1. In a suitable work area chalk a line for setting out the models.
2. Set out mortar spots and bricks in a symmetrical manner three bricks away from and parallel to the line of the models.
3. Set up profiles five bricks apart. Use dry bricks and chalk to measure the

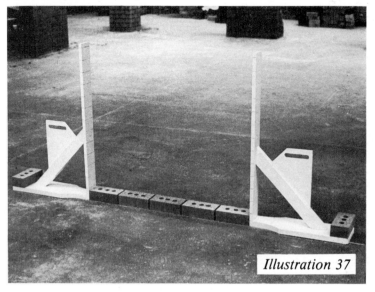

Illustration 37

required brick and cross-joint length of a five-brick-long wall. (Note that the profiles butt directly against the bricks.)

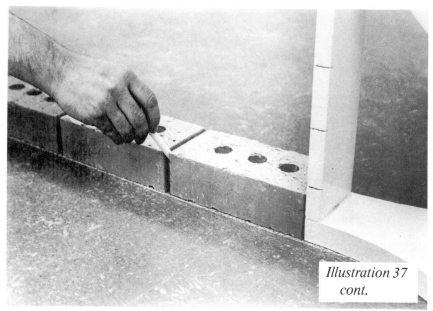

Illustration 37 cont.

4. Using blocks fix a bricklayer's line between the profiles to the gauge of the first course. It may be necessary to weight the profiles due to the tension on the line.
5. Start at the right-hand profile if a right-handed bricklayer and reversed if left-handed. Lay a mortar bed for one brick. Concentrate on obtaining approximately 12 mm thickness of bed at the edges and a deep centre furrow.

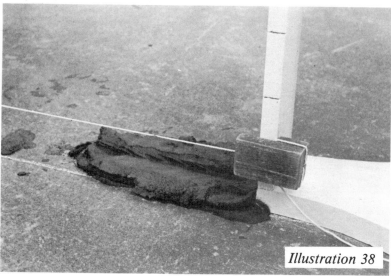

Illustration 38

6. Bed one brick dry against the profile with the front top arris level with and 0.5 mm behind the bricklayer's line.

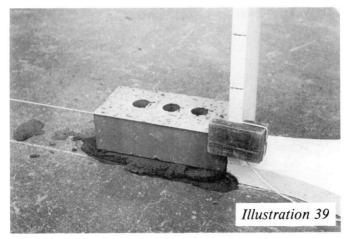

Illustration 39

7. Check by eye that the face of the bricks is vertical and adjust as necessary.
8. Lay the mortar bed for the second brick as before.
9. Pick up and butter the second brick. Bed the brick forming a 10-mm cross joint and lining the top arris level with and 0.5 mm behind the bricklayer's line.
10. Continue until the first course of bricks is laid. If the last brick will not fit do not adjust the profiles or cut the brick, take up such bricks as necessary and re-lay with the correct thickness of cross joint.
11. Lay a bed of mortar for the first half brick of the second course making sure that the bed averages 12 mm thickness at the edge, is well furrowed and has the surplus cut away from the brick.
12. Start the second course with a half brick making sure that the half brick

Illustration 40

butts dry against the profile and allows the formation of a cross joint central over the brick below. Cut surplus mortar away from the brickwork.

13. Complete the course as in 10, finishing with a half brick.
14. Continue the work until eight courses are completed.

Illustration 40 cont.

Marking scheme	
Evenness of bed joint thickness	10
Regularity of cross-joint widths	10
Verticality of face of bricks	5
Position of cross joints over course below (bonding)	10
Alignment of face plane	10
Cleanliness of face of bricks	5
Total	50

In this exercise the profiles determine the plumb, level and gauge and therefore they should be accurate. Careful attention must be paid to aligning the top arris of the bricks, to the vertical face of the bricks and to the cross-joint widths. If this is correctly executed the bed joints will be of even thickness, the face plane will be accurately alignable and bond will be correctly maintained.

This exercise should be repeated until at least standard facework quality is comfortably achieved. Students can work in pairs but item 5 will have to be adjusted accordingly and the model increased to ten bricks long. It is expected that students will need to complete this model more than once.

Practice model 3   Plumbing and gauging half-brick wall

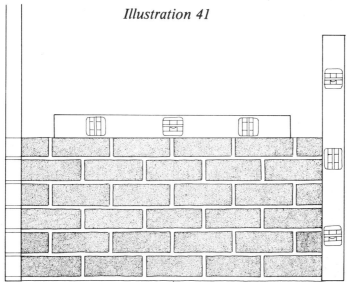

Illustration 41

Front elevation of model with checks for gauge, plumb and level

1. Prepare to start work as in Practice model 2.
2. Mark out the length of the wall along the setting out chalk line. Use dry bricks and chalk to measure a five-brick-long wall with allowance for cross joints.
3. Starting at the right- or left-hand end of the wall as appropriate lay a mortar bed of correct thickness for the first brick. Bed the first brick and press down to the gauge mark on the gauge lath.

Illustration 42

ISB - D

Check by eye that the brick is accurately aligned with the setting out marks and that the face of the brick is vertical.

If the brick is below the gauge mark take it up and re-lay it on a thicker bed.

4. Lay a bed for the second brick. Butter the cross joint of the second brick and lay it accurately along the setting out line forming a 10-mm cross joint between the two bricks.

5. Using the plumb level check that the first two bricks are level.

Illustration 43

6. Lay a bed at the opposite end of the wall, for one brick.
7. Lay the third brick to gauge and check as for the first brick.

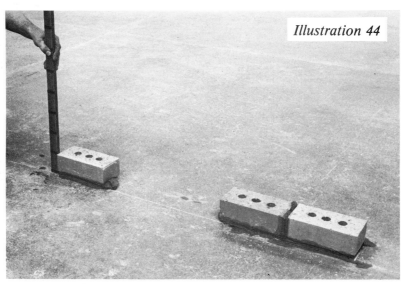

Illustration 44

8. Lay a bed for, butter the cross joint and lay a fourth brick against the third and accurately aligned with the setting out line.
9. Using the plumb level check the alignment, plumb and level of the four bricks laid.

Illustration 45

10. Lay bed and cross joints for the fifth brick. Form the cross joints by buttering the ends of the bricks already laid.

Illustration 46

11. Lay the fifth brick.

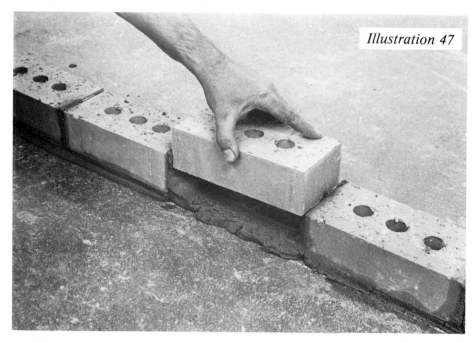

Illustration 47

12. Using the plumb level make a final check for alignment and level.

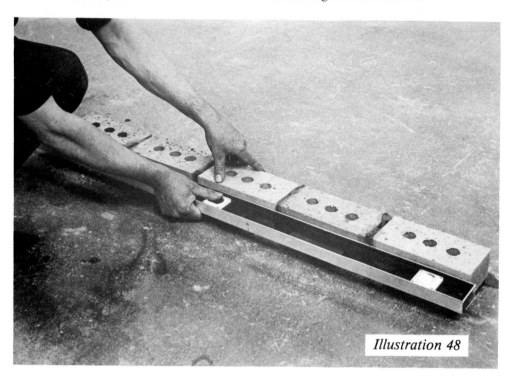

Illustration 48

13. Repeat the operations on the next course starting with a half brick. Use the plumb level additionally to check the alignment of the first one and a half bricks of the course by setting it at an angle against the face of the opposite end brick of the course below.

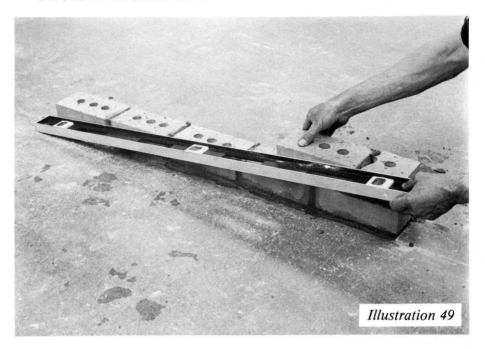

Illustration 49

14. Complete six courses.

Marking scheme	
Plumbing at ends and face (four plumbing points)	10
Accuracy gauge	10
Accuracy of level	10
Alignment of face plane	10
Thickness of bed joints	5
Thickness of cross joints	5
Total	50

To achieve a satisfactory standard adequate time should be taken to build this model. Gauging, plumbing, levelling and aligning the bricks is practiced on each course.

Accurate thickness of bed and cross joints are important prior to bedding the bricks. Work already completed will be disturbed if an error has to be corrected.

Bricks should not be cut or moved to allow the last brick of each course to be laid. This will be avoided if the half bricks and cross joints are accurately formed so that each cross joint is 10mm thick and central above the stretcher below it.

The finished model should be to gauge at each course to within 3mm.

Plumbing and level can be checked with the plumb level. It should be the case that in any plumbed or levelled section each brick should touch the plumb level.

The model may have to be built more than once to achieve a satisfactory standard.

Practice model 4   Half brick right-angled quoin, stopped end and raking back

Illustration 50

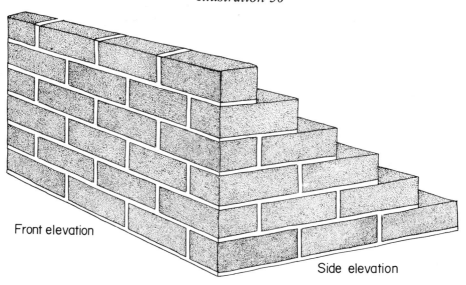

Front elevation

Side elevation

Isometric perspective of model

1. Chalk a line for setting out the models.
2. Set out mortar spots and bricks suitably spaced for the line of models.
3. Mark out the position of the models using a builder's square to form a right angle and dry bricks with 10-mm joints to establish the length of each elevation.
4. Bed the first brick at the quoin on the front elevation. Check the accuracy of gauge, plumb and level.

5. Cross joint and bed second, third and fourth bricks along the front elevation. Use the plumb level to check level and alignment.

Illustration 51

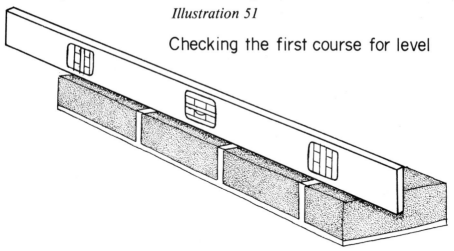

Checking the first course for level

6. Cross joint and bed the fifth and sixth bricks using the plumb level to check level and alignment.
7. Bed the first brick of the second course at the quoin. Check the accuracy of the gauge, plumb and level.
8. Bed the half brick at the stopped end on the front elevation and, using the plumb level, check the accuracy of level from the quoin to the stopped end.

Illustration 52

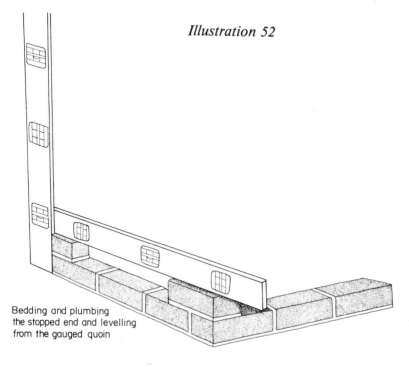

Bedding and plumbing the stopped end and levelling from the gauged quoin

9. Plumb the half bricks at the stopped end and on the front elevation.
10. Bed the brick abutting the half-brick stopped end taking care not to disturb the half brick by having too thick a cross joint on the brick as it is bedded. Using the plumb level check the brick for level and alignment between the quoin and the half-brick stopped end.

Illustration 53

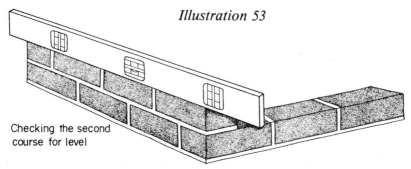

Checking the second
course for level

11. Bed the remaining bricks on the second course of the front elevation and check for level and alignment.
12. Lay the remaining bricks of the course on the side elevation and check for level and alignment on the face and for accuracy of lap at the raking back (i.e. the brick would allow a cross joint to be formed *central* above the brick below).
13. Complete five courses raking back along the side elevation at each course and checking the line of the raking back of each course.

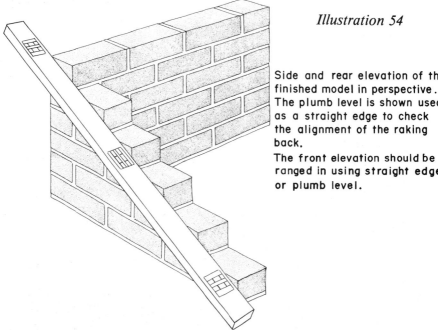

Illustration 54

Side and rear elevation of the finished model in perspective. The plumb level is shown used as a straight edge to check the alignment of the raking back.

The front elevation should be ranged in using straight edge or plumb level.

Marking scheme	
Plumbing:	
Stopped end	10
Stopped end front elevation	10
Quoin front elevation	10
Quoin side elevation	10
Level	10
Gauge	10
Cross joints	5
Bed joints	5
Cleanliness of bricks on face	10
Alignment of face plane	10
Accuracy of setting out right angle	10
Total	100

This model introduces raking back from a quoin. It is important that the bond of each course is correctly maintained, i.e. that each cross joint is central above the brick below. If this is not done and the quoin were part of a continuous wall the bricks used for completing each course between the raking back at each end of the wall would not fit correctly in the space.

This model requires close attention to plumbing at the stopped end and the quoin. Each brick should touch the plumb level. Bed and cross joints should be left rough from the trowel but well filled. The bricks should be left clean with no smudging on the face. To help to achieve full cross joints the buttering of the brick to be layed can be supplemented by skimming a small quantity of mortar on the cross-joint-face arris of the brick already layed.

Illustration 55

The use of dry bricks to check the overall size and shape of the model and as an aid to marking out is essential and should always be done prior to the final accurate marking out of a model.

Practice model 5   One brick wall in English bond

Illustration 56

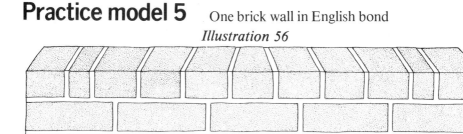

Front elevation of model in perspective

1. Chalk a line, set out material and mark the position of the model.
2. Using dry bricks accurately mark the overall dimensions of the model. Ensure that the thickness of the wall is not more or less than the length of one brick.

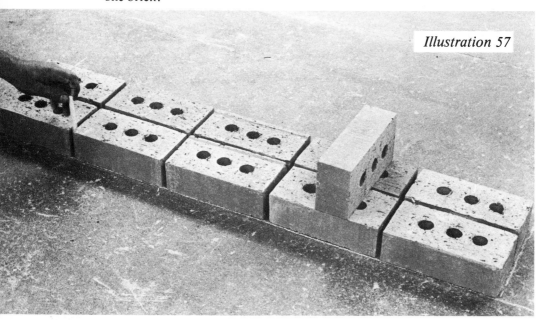

Illustration 57

3. Lay the first stretcher of the first course at one end of the front elevation of the model.
   Check for accurate gauge plumb and level.
4. Lay the second stretcher at the opposite end of the front elevation of the model and check the level from the first stretcher layed. Plumb the face and end of the second brick layed.

Illustration 58

5. Using line blocks or the method illustrated above fix a line and complete the front elevation of the first course of stretchers and check the level and alignment.
6. Lay the bed for the rear elevation of the first course of stretchers. Be sure that the bed averages 12 mm thick.
7. Draw the trowel point along behind the front elevation stretchers to form an additional furrow.

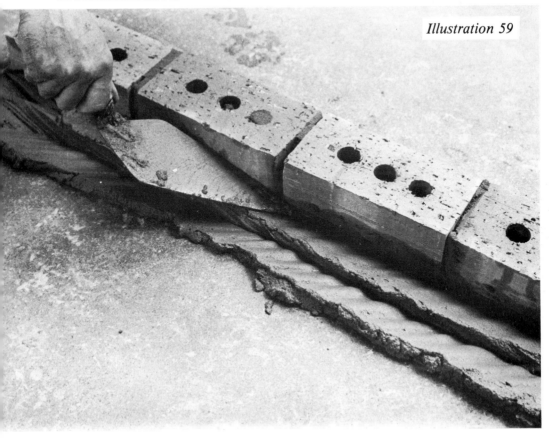

Illustration 59

8. Lay the rear elevation of the first course of stretchers. Check for level, alignment and width.

Illustration 60

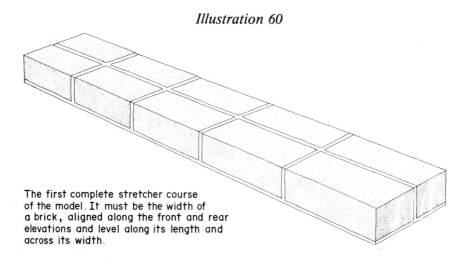

The first complete stretcher course
of the model. It must be the width of
a brick, aligned along the front and rear
elevations and level along its length and
across its width.

9. Build up one end of the model with a header closer and header on the second course, stretcher on the third course and a header on the fourth course. Check for gauge, level, plumb, ranging in width as the work proceeds.

Illustration 61

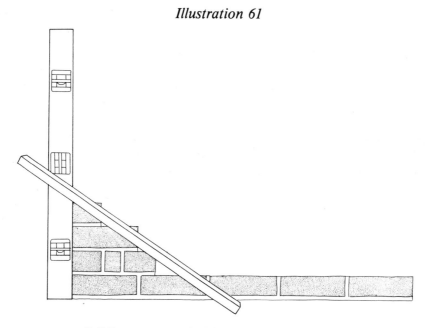

Building up one end of the model.

10. Repeat at the other end of the model.
11. Using bricklayer's lines on the front elevation of the model complete the four courses.

    As the back of the stretcher course is layed make sure that the mortar bed is furrowed clear of the back of the bricks already layed on that course.

    As the headers are layed make sure that they are level across the width of the wall.

Marking scheme	
Setting out including squareness of ends	10
Plumbing face and ends (plumbing 6 points)	10
Gauge	10
Level	10
Size of closers and accuracy of bonding	10
Width of cross joints	10
Thickness of bed joints	10
Face plane	10
Cleanliness of bricks and filling of bed and cross joints	10
General appearance including back	10
Total	100

This model demands accurate setting out and squaring of the ends on the first course.

The closers must be cut to the correct size (see Exercise 5). The headers and the back course of stretchers must be level across the width of the wall. The headers must be central over the cross joints or stretchers below.

The mortar beds must not be excessive or bricks will be difficult to lay to the correct gauge and level. The courses must be layed to a tight line but must not catch and distort it. The cross joints should be of uniform width and other than closers there should be no cutting of bricks.

It is not possible to plumb the back of the model, or to get a consistent rear face plane due to the differing lengths of bricks. The back, however, should be as consistent as possible with established standards. Stretcher courses should never protrude from the rear face.

Practice model 6
(unmarked)

Cavity quoin and reveal with horizontal and vertical damp-proof course and wall ties

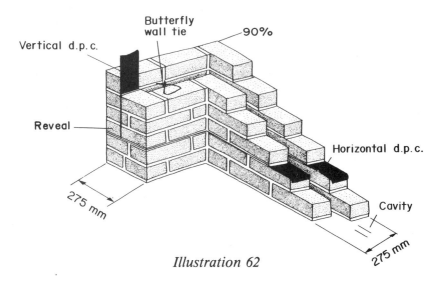

Illustration 62

This model is intended to develop students' ability to set out and cut for more intricate work at windows and door openings in cavity walls. It requires wall ties and damp-proof course.

The bricks for this first course should be cut and layed dry on setting out lines chalked out to the brick sizes and dimensions given.

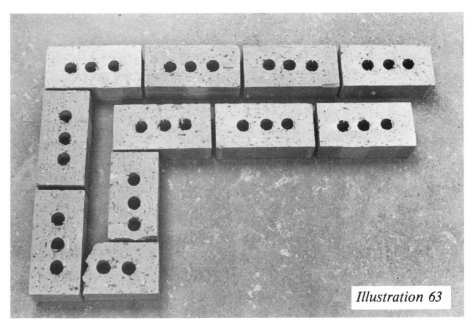

Illustration 63

The second course should be cut and layed dry over the first course keeping the bond, i.e. the cross joints of the second course central, over the bricks or cuts below, except at the cavity closing where the vertical damp-proof course occurs. The cut for the cavity closer at the reveal is measured to suit the space available and cut to allow a 10-mm cross joint adjacent to the brick and a direct abutment to the d.p.c.

*Illustration 63
cont.*

The first two courses of brickwork should be layed starting at the reveal on the face side and completing the face brickwork first.

After two courses horizontal damp-proof course is bedded on a 2-mm mortar bed. The vertical d.p.c. is slotted between the external and internal brick leaves at the reveal and three more courses of brickwork are completed. A wall tie is placed across the cavity as shown on the drawing and the model is then completed.

All plumbing levelling and gauging is done as necessary using skills already acquired.

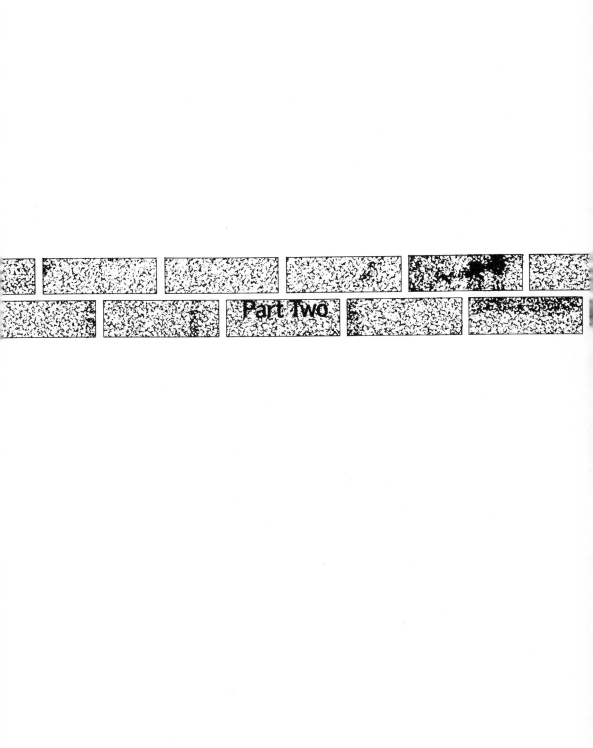

Part Two

8 Blocklaying

Blockwork

Blockwork is sometimes more suitable than brickwork and in certain cases is essential. In Britain, for example, cavity walls must have an inner leaf of suitable blocks to provide the necessary thermal insulation. For the specific qualities and structural performance of building blocks it is important to consult the manufacturer's specification. This text refers to solid blocks. Users need to check special applications of individual types before building with hollow blocks. Handling, bedding and cutting may vary substantially.

Blocklaying

Blocklaying is initially more difficult than bricklaying but it has the obvious advantage of taking less time to produce a similar area of wall. Because of its greater difficulty, blocklaying practice is beneficial and blocklaying will be more easily undertaken after the initial brickwork skills have been acquired.

Mortar

For practice purposes a 1 : 6 lime/sand mortar similar to that used for brickwork is suitable but the mix should be stiffer due to the greater weight of the blocks. The stiffer mortar provides a firm bed so that the blocks do not settle and lean out of plumb, but it follows that accurate bedding and placing is necessary because adjustment is more difficult. Practice and personal choice will determine the most suitable workability of the mortar.

Bedding

Blocks are layed on a 10-mm bed of mortar which is spread in the same way as for bricklaying.

57

Cross jointing

Many blocks have tongues and grooves. These should be fitted together. It is most convenient to strike the cross-joint mortar on to the last block layed. This is done by taking a trowel of mortar and drawing it across the vertical exposed arris of the block in a similar action to buttering the cross joint of a brick. A second action is used to butter the back vertical arris of the block.

Illustration 64

The cross joint can be buttered on the block to be layed, as with bricks, but this requires a firm bond between the mortar and the block. This is done by standing the block on its end and buttering the cross joint as though it were a furrowed bed joint. The furrow is trimmed to remove any excess and the block is lifted into place at an angle to avoid mortar falling off.

Illustration 65

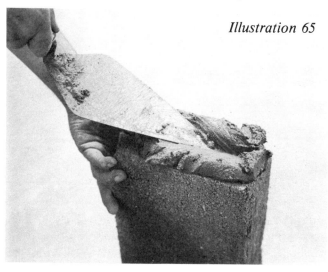

Handling blocks

Owing to the size and weight of blocks it is usual to lift them into position using both hands. There is no specific exercise which is useful in developing handling skills except to handle and appreciate the weight of the blocks to be layed.

Illustration 66

A two-handed grasp, in the manner illustrated above, is necessary to avoid the hands and fingers interfering with the cross joint or bedding.

As already stated, it is important to practice placing the block as near as possible to the final position due to the difficulty of adjusting its position. To make any final adjustments to the position of the block it is usual to use a lump hammer, again due to the weight of the block, however, blocks should not be struck so hard as to damage them. It is bad practice to move blocks which have become firmly bedded as this causes a permanent weakening of the mortar joints.

Cutting blocks

A bolster and lump hammer are used to cut blocks. The block is marked to the correct size of cut and placed on a soft fibreboard pad. The bolster is struck with a medium blow, moved along the cutting mark and struck again.

The bolster cutting is repeated on the back of the block and if necessary on the face again. This is continued until the block breaks.

Illustration 67

Any trimming of the cut block is done with the lump hammer and bolster which is struck down the cross-joint face. This method of trimming can be used to remove any unnecessary tongues on tongued and grooved blocks.

Bond

Blocks should be half bonded as in stretcher bond brickwork. When the blocks are used to form a quoin it is necessary to cut a quarter block to maintain correct bonding.

Illustration 68

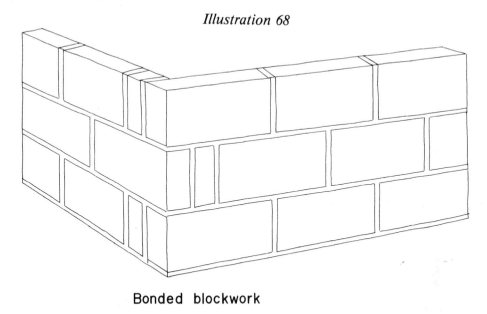

Bonded blockwork

Standards of accuracy

Blockwork is guaged, plumbed, levelled and layed to the bricklayer's lines as is brickwork.

Though blockwork is often plastered, i.e. unseen work, there is considerable advantage in high standards of accuracy. The blockwork is structurally more stable and produces a better surface for later surface treatment, e.g. plaster, paint.

From the blocklayer's standpoint it is quicker to build when blocks can easily be bedded to a line on a level bed provided by the previous, accurately layed course. When cross joints and bond are accurate cuts on alternate courses can be made to the same consistent dimensions as a single operation.

The gauge for blockwork may have to be adjusted to suit brickwork to which it is tied or bonded. The standard gauge is three courses of bricks to one course of blocks.

Where blockwork is used as the inner leaf of a cavity wall it is tied to the outer brickwork leaf with galvanised metal wall ties spaced 900 mm horizontally and 450 mm vertically, i.e. averaging one tie every second block every second course of blocks.

At points where the cavity is closed and a vertical damp-proof course occurs ties should be placed at every course of blockwork.

Practice model   Brick and block cavity wall

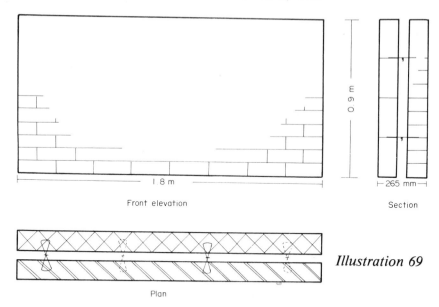

Front elevation   Section

Illustration 69

Plan

1. Set out the model according to brick and block sizes and dimensions given.
2. Lay the first course of bricks and of blocks, including all cuts, dry.
3. Bed and lay the first, second and third course of bricks to at least standard facework quality.
4. Working from the opposite side of the model bed and lay the first course of blocks.
5. Set wall ties tails down and central in the cavity between the external and internal leafs at the correct distances and build a further six courses of brickwork.

Illustration 70

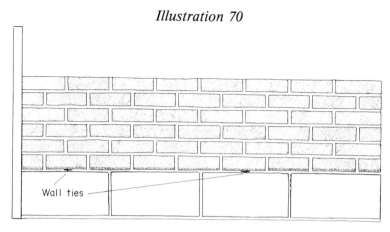

Wall ties

Rear elevation

6. From the opposite side of the model build two courses of blockwork and set wall ties between the external and internal leafs at the correct distances apart but staggered between the lower ties.
7. Complete the brickwork and blockwork of the model.

Marking scheme	
Setting out including width of cavity and overall width of wall	10
Plumbing on face brickwork	10
Plumbing on blockwork	10
Gauge of brickwork	10
Level between brickwork and blockwork courses at wall tie and finished heights	10
Brickwork face plane	10
Blockwork face plane	10
Uniformity of thickness and width of bed and cross joints. Brickwork and blockwork	10
Accuracy of cutting blocks and half bonding	10
Cleanliness of cavity and position of wall ties	10
Total	100

This practice model incorporates cavity and wall ties and represents a typical structural cavity wall for domestic purposes in Britain.

The brickwork of the external leaf should be at least to standard facework quality and the blockwork should have plumbing, levelling and face plane accuracy of at least common brickwork quality.

All bed and cross joints should be completely filled when left rough from the trowel. At this practice stage it should be unnecessary to fill except very occasionally. The completely filled joints help when jointing or pointing (see page 75).

The purpose of the cavity is to prevent moisture passing from the outside of the building. The cavity must not be bridged by mortar lodging on the wall ties or falling to the bottom and filling the cavity above any horizontal damp-proof course there may be.

The cavity is kept clean by careful bedding and cleaning off inside the cavity, the use of timber laths resting on the cavity ties to catch the mortar which falls and by removal of fallen mortar through holes made by leaving out bricks at the bottom of the wall. All or any combination of these methods can be used to keep the cavity clean. In the case of this model cleaning holes are unnecessary.

Final model
(unmarked)

Common and facing brick and block cavity wall with horizontal and vertical damp-proof courses, and cavities closed for door and window openings

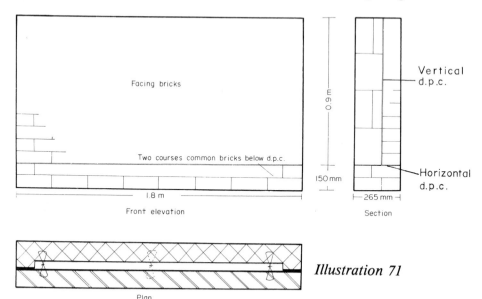

Illustration 71

1. Set out for and lay first two courses of common brickwork. Check that the setting out suits block and facing brick dimensions. Leave one or more bricks out of the bottom course for cleaning the cavity if required.
2. Position the profile at one end of the brickwork in the same position as a timber door or window frame would be set. (Usually 25 mm back from the face of the brickwork.) Mark the gauge on the profile.

Illustration 72

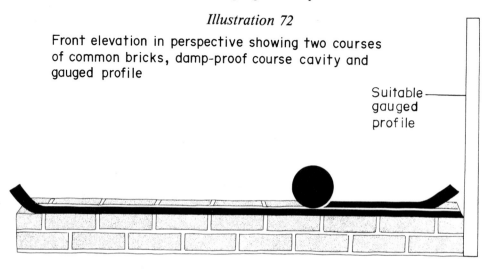

3. Roll out the horizontal damp-proof course on approximately 2-mm-thick mortar bed making any necessary cuts to cover the whole of the brickwork. Lap the d.p.c. a distance at least equal to its width (in this case 100 mm).

4. Build up three courses of raking back brickwork at each end of the model using plumb face level and profile as appropriate. Fix vertical damp-proof course.

Illustration 73

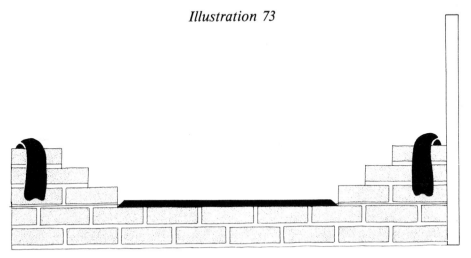

Front elevation

5. Using bricklayer's line run in the three courses of face brickwork.

6. Cut two block cavity closers and two quarter blocks to suit block half-bond requirements.

Illustration 74

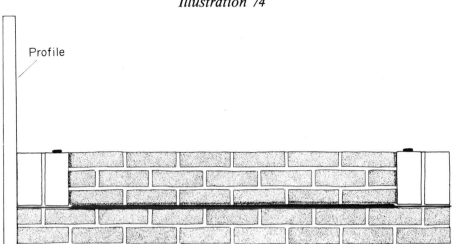

Rear elevation

7. Bed the block cavity closers and quarter blocks at end of the internal leaf.
8. Using bricklayer's line 'run in' the course of blocks.
9. Place wall ties at each end of the model 250 mm from the external end faces and along the length of the model at approximately 900 mm.
10. Build up six courses of raking back face brickwork at each end of the model *including a wall tie* each end immediately above the lower wall ties after these courses have been layed.

Illustration 75

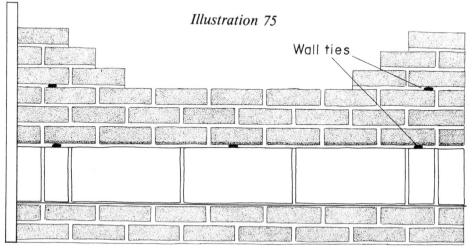

Rear elevation

11. Run in the six courses of face brickwork using a bricklayer's line. Include wall ties as necessary to satisfy the requirements of accuracy described on page 61.
12. Cut the necessary block cavity closers and quarter blocks for raking back two courses of blockwork at each end and build up the ends and return in blockwork. Take care not to disturb the brickwork where the wall tie is built in. Note that block cavity closers include cavity width (50 mm) closers on the second, fourth, etc., courses of blocks, laid adjacent to full blocks.

Illustration 76

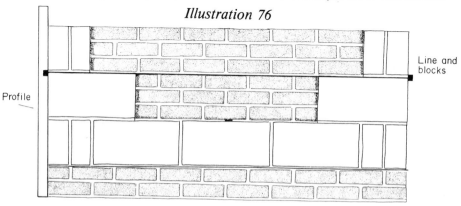

Rear elevation

13. Run the two courses of blockwork using a bricklayer's line.
14. Place wall ties at each end of the model as in item 9 above and along the length of the model at approximately 900 mm but staggered between the ties below.
15. Complete the model to the height shown in the drawing.
16. Joint up the face brickwork as described on pages 72, 73, 74.

General note

It is important not to disturb brickwork or bedded wall ties to accommodate blocks or bricks.

In the model above if rigid wall ties are used it would be beneficial to bed another block at each end of the model after 9, so that disturbance of work is avoided.

In cavity walling in normal circumstances one leaf of the wall should not rise more than 450 mm above the other.

The student should have no difficulty in preparing a marking scheme for this model based on establishing skills and standards of finished work.

By this time individual preferences for hand skills and methods of working will be developing. In so far as these do not interfere with neat, accurate, precise and quick workmanship it is in order for these different approaches to be used to the benefit of the individual student.

9 Jointing and Pointing

Tools

For execution of these two operations a jointing iron and a pointing trowel are required in addition to a bricklaying trowel.

Jointing

This is the term used for tool finishing the bed and cross joint mortars of brickwork and blockwork as the work proceeds. The illustration below shows a typical jointing iron used for this purpose.

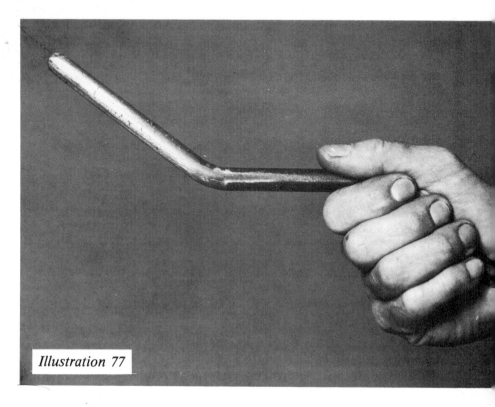

Illustration 77

Pointing

This term refers to finishing the bed and cross joints by filling and tooling the joints on completion of the work. It usually means raking out the existing mortar to a depth of 12 mm (in the case of old work chiselling out) and filling with a special or different mortar using a pointing trowel.

Immediately prior to pointing old work the brickwork should be thoroughly wetted. Wetting and pointing should be done in 1 m² areas.

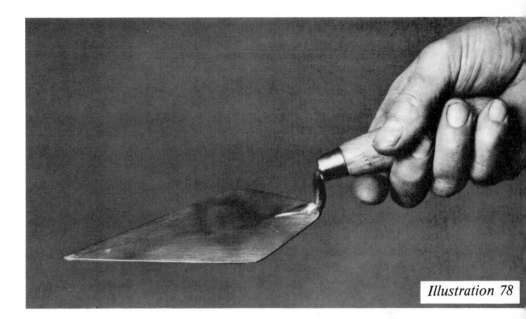

Illustration 78

Mortars

Bedding mortar used for practice or permanent work is satisfactory for jointing the finished work. In both cases the jointing should be completed after the mortar has stiffened due to water absorption into the bricks but before the mortar begins to set.

For pointing permanent work a mortar similar to the original should be used at a strength in most cases of not less than 1 : 1 : 6 cement/lime/sand nor greater than 1 : 4 cement/sand.

Filling joints

It must be emphasised that jointing and pointing should not be attempted before satisfactory standards of finished brickwork for practice model 5 have been achieved. By this time the practice of leaving adequately filled mortar joints rough from the trowel should be well established.

Illustration 79

Well-filled joints left rough from the trowel

Any supplementary joint filling should be done at this stage with a pointing trowel used to pick the mortar from the back of the bricklaying trowel blade, transfer the mortar to the joint and press home.

The mortar, which is stiffer than for bedding bricks, is flattened over the blade of the bricklaying trowel to a thickness of 10mm. This allows mortar to

Illustration 80

be pressed into 10-mm joints without smudging the brick arris or face.

Illustration 80
cont.

Fill all the cross and bed joints in the area to be filled before jointing is started.

Jointing cross joints

All the cross jointing in the area to be jointed should be completed before the bed joints are started.

For iron jointing the 15-mm-diameter jointing iron, usually made from twice cranked steel pipe, is held vertically and drawn with an even pressure down, or where convenient up, the line of the cross joint.

Illustration 81

The depth of the jointing should be the same irrespective of the width of the joint between the bricks. If a joint is pressed too deeply refill the joint and repeat the operation.

Cross joints should be vertical over each other but there is sometimes variation between courses. It is possible to reduce the apparent variation by using the plumb level as a straight edge to guide the line of movement of the jointing iron. The plumb rule is used to get best compromise line not necessarily the plumb line.

Illustration 82

Jointing bed joints

All bed joints should be filled in the same manner as cross joints.

Jointing is carried out by running the jointing iron along the face of the mortar in a long, even, continuous movement of about 750 mm at a time. The joint may require a second sweep of the iron but polishing the mortar should be avoided.

As with cross joints the depth of the jointing should be the same irrespective of the thickness of the bed joint. If a joint is pressed too deeply refill and repeat the operation.

Bed joints should be horizontal and it is possible to improve the line of jointing by using the plumb level as a straight edge to guide the jointing iron.

Illustration 83

After jointing there will be minor blemishes due to protruding mortar deposits on the bed and cross joints. After the mortar joints are past their initial drying out these blemishes should be removed by brushing with a soft brush. Excessive brushing, brushing with a hard brush or brushing before the initial drying out will produce unsightly marks on the mortar joints and adjacent bricks (see illustration 86).

Pointing cross and bed joints

The raked out cross and bed joints are filled as previously described filling cross then bed joints in that order using the bricklaying and pointing trowels.

The joints are trowelled with the pointing trowel by pressing the blade so that the outer surface is flush with the face of the brick above and the back of the blade runs along the arris of the brick below the joint to form a weather edge.

Illustration 84

The apparent plumb and level of the joints can be enhanced by marking the weather edge of the pointing with the trowel point guided as necessary by the plumb level.

Illustration 85

Illustration 86

10 Permanent Work

SPEEDS of bricklaying after completion of these exercises and models will be very much below that achieved by fully skilled bricklayers. Extensive practice is required before high-quality brickwork is achieved as a matter of course. Students should be aware of their limitations when considered against the criteria set out in Section 2.

With this in mind students will nonetheless be able to undertake some sort of permanent work before or on completion of all the models in this book. The best students may find that they can satisfactorily complete good-quality facing brickwork, others may find unseen brickwork more suitable for their levels of skill.

It is sensible to use foundation work or other unseen brickwork for further practice. Students could therefore embark on such brickwork with a view to improving skills to a level suitable for any seen or facing brickwork which may be part of the same building.

Permanent work discussed here is limited to domestic work such as garden walls garages and two-storey housing. It is assumed that any necessary permission for the work to be undertaken will be dealt with by others and it is therefore outside the scope of this book. Similarly, technical aspects of brick structures such as foundation depths, structural stability, load bearing capacity, resistance to moisture, thermal efficiency, etc., are a matter for reference elsewhere.

This section is concerned with setting out, mortar mixes and bricks suitable for brickwork in small-scale domestic work.

Mortars

Sand

For bricklaying mortar it is important that bricklaying sand is used, i.e. a sand with a suitable mix of graded particles which are not too sharp or angular.

77

The sand must be clean, free from salts, loam or vegetable matter and preferably washed.

Cement

Cement should normally be Ordinary Portland cement but in some cases special cements are necessary to resist attack from water-borne impurities which will damage the hardened mortar. If in doubt take advice on this point from experienced builders about special cements or additives to cement which should be used in particular localities.

Masonry cement is a common alternative to Ordinary Portland cement and saves the addition of lime to the mortar mix. The masonary cement has been processed so that it improves the workability and plasticity of the freshly mixed mortar in the same way as the addition of lime.

Lime

Lime is non-hydraulic, i.e. not having fully absorbed the water needed in the hardening process.

Water

Water used for bricklaying mortars should be clean and drinkable.

Mortar mixes

For brickwork below ground level a $1 : \frac{1}{2} : 4\frac{1}{2}$ cement : lime : sand mix is usually satisfactory. The cement-rich mix helps resistance to frost action and moisture penetration. This richer mix should be used up to the horizontal damp-proof course placed at 150 mm above ground level.

Above the horizontal d.p.c. a $1 : 1 : 6$ cement : lime : sand mix is acceptable. This mix is more flexible and allows for movement of the brickwork due to expansion and contraction caused by heat and moisture. An alternative mix would be $1 : 4\frac{1}{2}$ masonry cement : sand.

When brickwork is particularly exposed, e.g. the top courses of a garden wall where moisture and frost penetrate from both sides and the top, a cement-rich mix is needed. The mortar mix for brickwork below ground level would be appropriate in this case or as an alternative a $1 : 3$ masonary cement : sand mix.

It will be noted that from a practical viewpoint the different mortars have different trowel characteristics. This will require minor adjustments in trowel techniques and bedding.

Mixing mortar

For small works hand mixing is convenient and cheap. The cement lime and sand are measured by volume using a builder's shovel. The dry materials are put into a single heap and then shovelled in their entirety to a second heap. This is repeated so that the material is transferred from one heap to another three times and a thorough mix of the dry materials is achieved.

Illustration 87

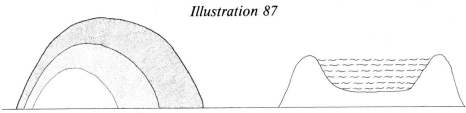

Sand, cement and lime transferred three times

Dry materials spread and water added before final mixing to the required consistency

The dry materials are then spread to form a hollow into which water is poured and mixed until a mortar of suitable consistency is produced, care should be taken to stop water running from the materials and washing cement powder away.

Machine-mixed mortars are usually more consistent than hand-mixed mortars. Using a machine the first mix may be lean, i.e. short of cement due to the internal surface of the mixer drum being coated. This is overcome by adding a small extra amount of cement.

Machine mixing is done by putting half the required water into the drum, adding the required cement lime and sand in that order and then the remaining water.

In the above cases the use of a shovel as a gauge for dry materials is satisfactory but should not be considered as good practice for specialised structural brickwork. In any event, care should be taken to ensure that similar sized shovels are used for the different materials.

Bricks

Bricks are available in three broad varieties and qualities. Common, engineering and facing varieties may be of internal, ordinary or special quality.

This means that it is possible to have a facing brick which is only suitable for internal work, a common brick which has special qualities or an engineering brick which is of common variety.

In view of the possible combinations of appearance, weathering, moisture absorption, load-bearing capacity and density of bricks it is important to consider the characteristics required of bricks for a particular purpose.

Ordinary quality common

Illustration 89

This class 5 common brick has a smooth even surface which could be considered as producing an attractive finish. Owing to its lower density and higher water absorption, i.e. ordinary quality, it is not suitable for exposed brickwork where moisture and freezing can weather off the face of the brick.

An unprotected brick of ordinary quality may be unsuitable for garden walls due to moisture and frost attack at ground level, on both sides and on top of the wall. It could safely be used above a horizontal d.p.c. and below a moisture-resistant weather capping in the main body of a wall.

Special quality common

Illustration 88

This perforated common brick is dense, resistant to moisture absorption and has a high crushing strength. For domestic work its strength is substantially in excess of loads carried. Its resistance to moisture and frost attack makes it suitable for brickwork likely to suffer these effects at or near ground level and at the top of walls.

Bricks like this could be used from two courses below the ground to two courses above the ground on any wall to form a band of four courses of weather resisting brickwork at these critical points.

When laid on edge the bricks would be suitable for weather capping.

Special quality facing

Illustration 90

This facing brick is of the same quality as the previously illustrated engineering brick but has dragfaced rustications. Weathered rusticated bricks should be layed weathering downwards. Facing bricks of this quality can be used in the same positions as special quality engineering bricks but the rustications are likely to suffer frost damage when the bricks are used as a wall capping.

Ordinary quality facing

Illustration 91

A typical ordinary quality class 3 facing brick such as this is suitable for walls in conditions of normal exposure, e.g. garage walls, the internal and external leaf of cavity walls, internal decorative brickwork, garden walls with suitable d.p.c. and capping.

For permanent brickwork or blockwork to give longest life and usefulness with the least maintenance it is important to choose the correct brick for the purpose and bed the bricks in the most suitable mortar.

The foregoing illustrations and comments are very brief and are intended to offer the most basic information which can be used as a guide when choosing bricks.

Note particularly that the appearance, method of manufacture, number of holes, type of frog, surface finish, etc., do not necessarily determine the quality or performance of a brick.

Coloured Mortars

The colour of a mortar used with a particular brick can have a marked effect on the appearance of the finished brickwork. It is, therefore, important to consider the final appearance of the work when the bricks and mortar are dried. To establish the appearance of the bricks and mortar to be used a small sample panel of two bricks bedded together can be dried with a blow lamp.

Sands of naturally different colours will produce different coloured mortar, red sands tending to produce darker mortar than yellow sands. Note that richer cement mix will produce a darker mortar but cement/sand ratio must be determined by other considerations.

If the natural colour of the mortar is unsatisfactory colouring agents can be added. It is essential that manufacturer's instructions are followed when these agents are added as small variations in mix quantities can cause marked colour variations.

The most consistent artificial colouring is obtained by using ready mixed coloured mortars which only need the addition of cement. The whole of the bedding mortar should be coloured so that as weathering occurs the colour is consistent through the thickness of the wall. For repointing in coloured mortar this method of bedding is not available.

Joints

Pointing and jointing techniques will also affect the appearance of the finished work and the practice described on pages 68–76 does not extend beyond the most common methods.

It should be noted that the type of joint finish affects the amount of exposure to weathering, the most marked example being a raked-out joint which leaves the arrises of the brick fully exposed. In this and some other cases the quality of the bricks used would need to take account of the additional exposure.

For more detailed information see Construction Industry Training Board Standard Scheme of Training, pages 85–86 (Further Reading).

Tools

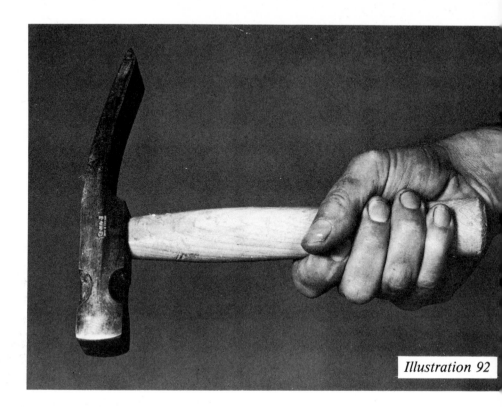

Illustration 92

Brick hammer

A brick hammer is not essential for cutting bricks and there are two points to be remembered if it is used:
1. The level of visual and manual co-ordination must be well developed to avoid injury and to cut bricks successfully.
2. The accuracy of cutting is reduced.

If it is considered that a brick hammer is a worthwhile expense and its use will not produce too low a standard of cutting, the advantage is that a brick hammer will save time. Practice can waste bricks and it is recommended that for such practice old or broken bricks are used. The cuts are achieved by striking the bricks with a firm blow. As with other bricklaying skills practice will improve performance.

No exercises are described here but various uses of the brick hammer are illustrated.

Illustration 93

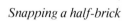

Snapping a half-brick

Cutting a three-quarter brick

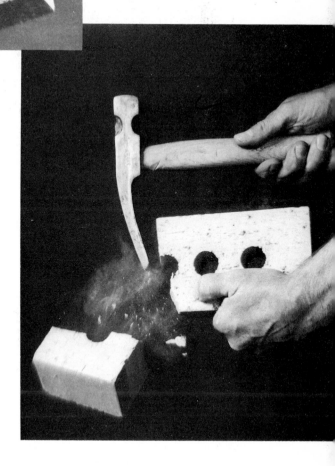

*Illustration 93
  cont.*
        Trimming a cut to size

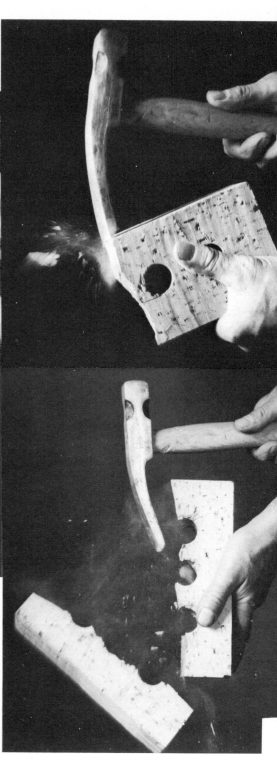

*Cutting a king closer
(see bond details of
quoin, illustration 96)*

Cutting a queen closer

Tingle

Illustration 94   *A metal tingle plate*

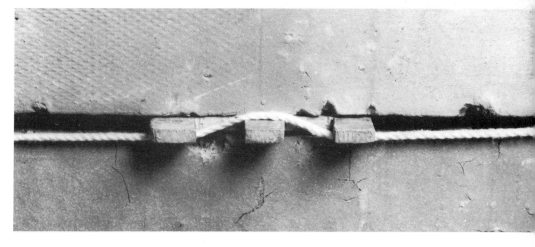

Bricklayer's line woven through
a tingle set to gauge

A tingle is an intermediate support to stop lines from sagging. It is often a
piece of card folded round the bricklayer's line and trapped under a brick.

Setting out for permanent work

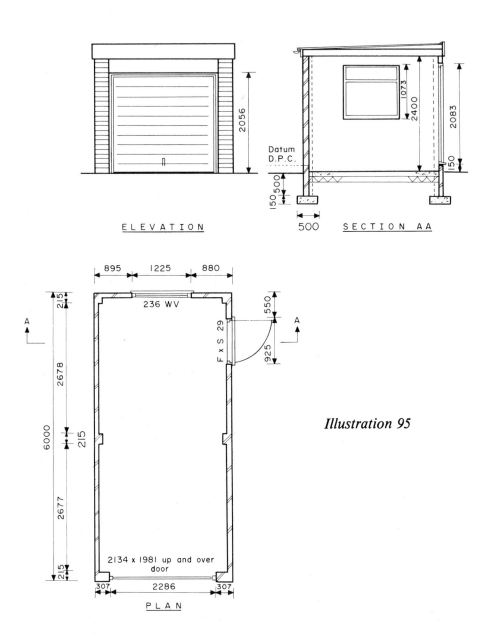

ELEVATION   500   SECTION AA

Illustration 95

PLAN

The drawings show details of a brick garage built on concrete strip found-ations and form the basis of the procedure described below for setting out the brickwork. With suitable adjustment this procedure can be used for most domestic brickwork. It is assumed that setting out and levelling for excavation and concreting is completed and the main building setting out lines are marked out at ground level. This exercise is concerned only with setting out the brickwork.

1. Study the drawing and note details which may affect the brickwork bonding arrangements or the finished size of the building. Pay attention particularly to the following.
   (a) Will multiples of brick and cross joints coincide with the dimensions given.
   (b) Will the door and window openings coincide with possible bonding arrangements.
   (c) Are the common and facing bricks the same size.
   (d) Does the foundation depth and the ground level gauge datum suit the brick gauge.

   Assuming that the dimension of the building are not rigidly fixed it is possible to consider and solve problems related to the above points during the course of construction of work below ground level. It is essential to be aware of possible difficulties.

2. Mark the position of the building on the foundation concrete by plumbing down from the setting out lines at ground level.
3. Check the dimensions marked on the foundation concrete for accuracy and square.
4. Set out and bond with dry brick the whole of the first course of common bricks including any cutting. Allow for 10-mm cross joints and measure these with the thickness of a piece of chalk.
5. At each stop end, quoin and pier dry bond the second course of bricks.
6. With chalk and using the door and window frames as a guide mark the positions of these openings in the brickwork on the concrete strip foundations.
7. Check items 1(a) and 1(b) against the dry layed and bonded brickwork and make any necessary adjustments to overall dimensions, positions of openings and bonding arrangement.
8. Starting at the quoin by the gauge datum bed the first bricks to gauge working down from the datum. Check item 1(d).
   To achieve correct gauge it may be necessary to squeeze the bed joints or to thicken them. Soften or stiffen the mortar as required. Try to avoid cutting bricks as this is time consuming but it may be necessary. It is important to get the top of the first course accurately gauged and levelled.
9. Build up the brickwork at the gauge datum stopped end and return quoin

to three courses below horizontal damp-proof course, i.e. one course below ground level. Rake back as necessary.

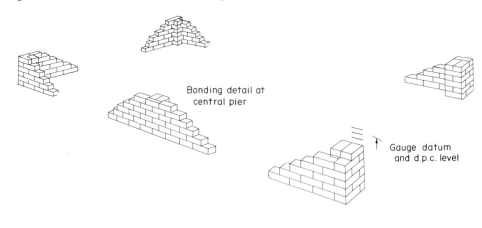

Bonding detail at central pier

Gauge datum and d.p.c. level

Stopped ends and quoins built up to one course below ground level

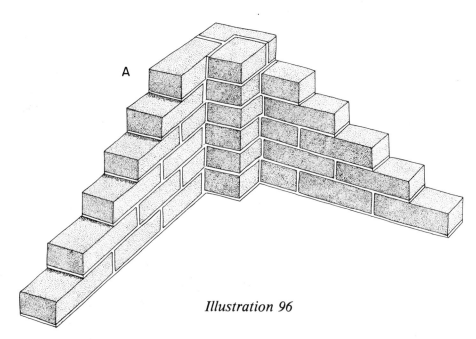

A

Illustration 96

Illustration of bond at rear quoin. The use of three-quarter brick and king closers is repeated at the front stopped end. For the centre pier a queen stretcher and two three-quarter bricks are used every second course.

10. Using plumb level and straight edge accurately bed to the correct level gauge and dimensions the bricks at the next quoin. Carefully check the accuracy of level, gauge and dimensions before proceeding.

11. Build up the brickwork at this quoin as in item 9 above.
12. Move to the next quoin and proceed as in item 10 above.
13. Complete the brickwork to one course below ground level using lines and tingles as necessary.

Mark the positions of the door and window frame using actual frame sizes.

Illustration 97

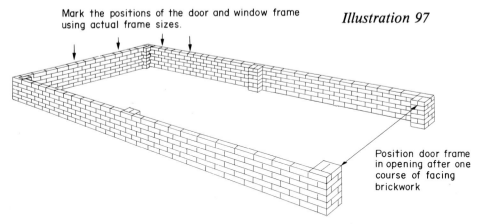

Position door frame in opening after one course of facing brickwork

Completed common brickwork below ground level

14. Check the setting out dimensions of the completed brickwork and using chalk re-mark the positions of the door and window openings.
    Using the plumb/level and long straight edge confirm level and accuracy of gauge.
15. Dry bond the first course of facing brickwork and check in the same manner as the common brickwork in items 4 and 5 above.

Frames plumbed and propped for profiles

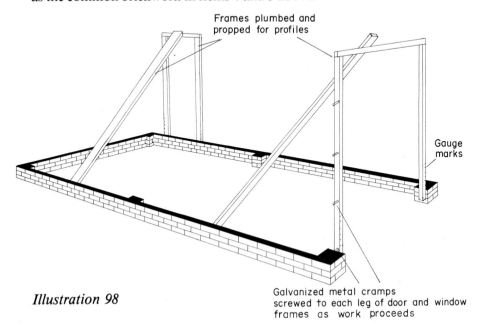

Gauge marks

Illustration 98

Galvanized metal cramps screwed to each leg of door and window frames as work proceeds

16. Make any necessary adjustments to squareness, dimensions, bond and gauge. It is acceptable to 'break' bond at this course. Any straight cross joints or other defects will not be seen and any weakening of the brickwork is not serious.

17. To a minimum of standard B complete the facing brickwork to and including horizontal d.p.c.

18. Fix the doors temporarily but accurately in position using props. Check for plumb on the face and sides and level across the top.

19. Using the doors as profiles and building in screwed galvanised door cramps as required build up the quoins at each corner of the building together with adjacent stop ends and piers to six courses high plumbing and levelling as necessary.

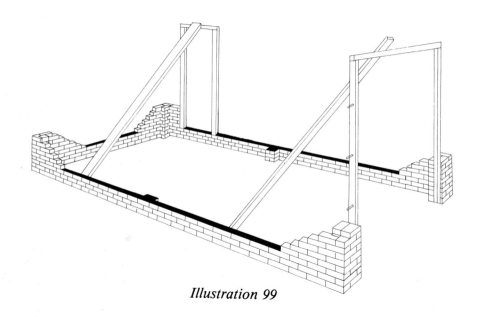

Illustration 99

Brickwork raked back
ready for running in

20. Run in the brickwork between the raking back and repeat items 19 and 20 consecutively until the work is up to window sill height. Set window frame in position and build in as door frames.

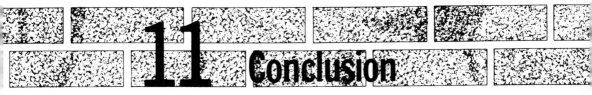

11 Conclusion

GIVEN sufficient practice most people are able to lay bricks to a satisfactory standard for ordinary purposes.

Bricklaying has many uses ranging from garden flower beds to multi-storey buildings.

To the individual, bricklaying is often a useful and satisfying activity which also produces the direct benefit of saving costs.

This book has set out an approach to the acquisition of the skills of brick-laying which will be useful for the individual self-taught student and for groups in education or vocational training who wish to improve their practical skills.

It is hoped that those who use it will enjoy developing those skills and marking their progress so that at some stage they will feel confident to produce high-quality permanent work which will be admired by those who see it.

The skills gained have use in many types of building work but typically small works round the house would be the first use of these skills. Boundary walls, screen walls, gate piers, paving and similar work will be within the ability of most students and these final photographs show work which they should be able to equal except illustration 104.

This boundary wall in FLEMISH English bond shows a simple decorative pattern. Adequate coping and damp-proof courses have protected the bricks from damage due to frost action and due to moisture rising from the ground. Students may consider the quality of finish less than satisfactory, in particular the bond below the decorative pattern.

Illustration 100

An old boundary wall

Illustration 101

Hydraulically pressed concrete walling, screen blocks and coping

Hydraulically pressed concrete walling is relatively dense, i.e. similar to bricks of special quality and in this case no d.p.c. is necessary. The screen wall blocks are protected by a concrete coping.

A half-brick-thick wall such as this will require piers or buttressing at intervals to stop it twisting over.

Protecting brickwork from the weather can be done by using more bricks of suitable quality which in themselves add decoration. This gate pier has a flexible d.p.c. 150 mm above ground level (not visible) and is capped with special quality smooth common bricks layed on edge. The top course of facing bricks have suffered moss staining due to the omission of a weather throating below the capping.

Illustration 102

Gate pier of rusticated facing bricks capped with special quality commons The bricklayer building this pier had a momentary lapse and layed some bricks the wrong way up.

Illustration 103

Paving using
215 × 105 × 50mm
brick paviors

This brick paving uses a simple but attractive pattern. In laying paving it is important to mark the setting out carefully using dry bricks. Lay the bricks to a line to ensure that the pattern does not creep because shape of the paving bricks cannot be relied on as a setting out guide.

Paving bricks are of special quality to British Standard 3921 Class 1 and any brick of similar quality can be used for paving. The bricks are usually bedded on 1:4 cement/sand mortar and the sub-base for paving should be at least 100 mm compacted hardcore.

As well as the pattern, levels and falls for drainage are also maintained by laying to a line. Students will note that the pattern illustrated allows only two out of three bricks to be layed directly to the line.

More complicated patterns, for example herringbone or radial paving, also need careful setting out and line work. Such work is outside the scope of this book but is not necessarily outside the scope of its readers.

Illustration 104

There is no book available with just the purpose of teaching bricklaying hand skills though there are many books on bricklaying and building which students might find helpful and interesting. In any case brickwork has a very long history and there are many examples to see. Possibly the first approach to finding out how a piece of brickwork is to be undertaken is to look at similar existing brickwork.

Further Reading

ARMOUR, M., *Building your own home*. Dorchester: Prism Press, 1980.

BAILEY, H., *Brickwork and associated studies*. London: Macmillan, 1979.

CONSTRUCTION INDUSTRY TRAINING BOARD, *Basic bricklaying: practical tests*. London: C.I.T.B., 1974.

DANIEL, R. A., *Brickwork and blockwork*. London: Newnes Technical Books, 1977.

DAY, R., *All about brickwork, stonework and concrete*. London: Hamlyn, 1976.

HODGE, J. C., *Brickwork for apprentices*. London: Edward Arnold, 1971.

JACKSON, A. and DAY, D., *Good Housekeeping D.I.Y. Book*. London: Ebury Press, 1977.

KNIGHT, T. L. *Illustrated introduction to brickwork design*. Windsor Brick Development Association, 1975.

McKAY, W. B., *Brickwork*. London: Longmans, 1974.

NASH, W. G., *Brickwork bonding problems and solutions*. London: Hutchinson, 1977.

NASH, W. G., *Brickwork*. London: Hutchinson, 1970.

SMITH, S., *Brickwork*. London: Macmillan, 1972.

WHITEHOUSE, T. R., *Working with bricks, concrete and stone*. London: Readers Digest Association, 1976.